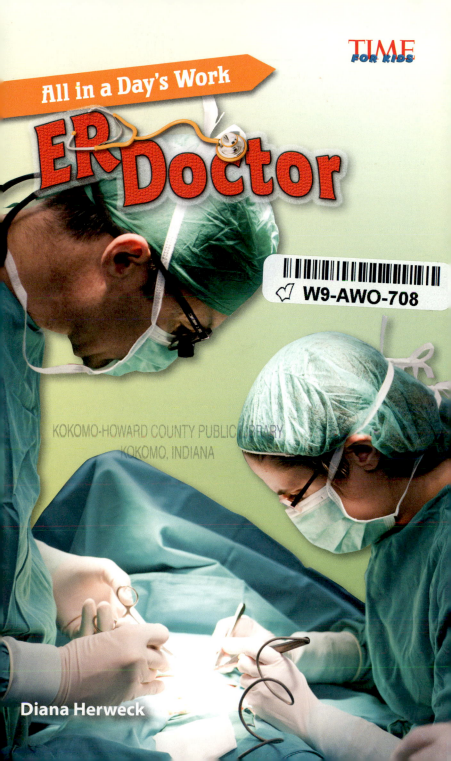

All in a Day's Work

TIME
FOR KIDS

ER Doctor

W9-AWO-708

Diana Herweck

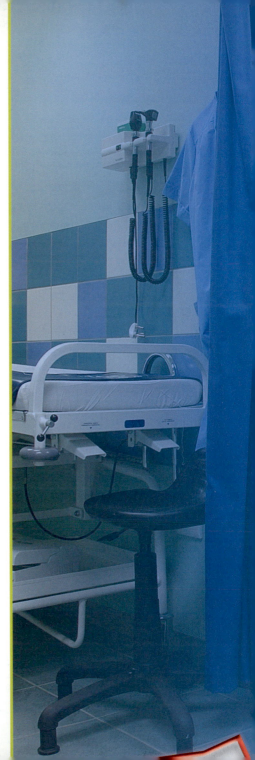

Consultants

Timothy Rasinski, Ph.D.
Kent State University

Lori Oczkus
Literacy Consultant

Byron Garibaldi, M.D.
ER Physician

Erin Hunter, M.D.
ER Physician

Based on writing from
TIME For Kids. *TIME For Kids* and the *TIME For Kids* logo are registered trademarks of TIME Inc. Used under license.

Publishing Credits

Dona Herweck Rice, *Editor-in-Chief*
Lee Aucoin, *Creative Director*
Jamey Acosta, *Senior Editor*
Courtney Patterson, *Designer*
Stephanie Reid, *Photo Editor*
Rane Anderson, *Contributing Author*
Rachelle Cracchiolo, *M.S.Ed., Publisher*

Image Credits: p.52 Bridgeman Art Library, pp.46–47 Getty Images, p.46 iStockphoto, pp.12–13 AFP/Getty Images/Newscom, pp.40–41 Newscom, p.36 FEATURECHINA/Newscom, pp.34–35 imagebroker/Jochen Tack/Newscom, pp.44–45 MCT/Newscom, pp.50–51 Xinhua/Photoshot, p.6 REUTERS/Newscom, pp.6–7 UPI/Newscom, pp.20, 20–21 The New York Times/Newscom, p.48 ZUMAPRESS.com/Newscom, pp.10, 22, 31, 43, 50–51 (illustrations) Timothy J. Bradley; All other images from Shutterstock.

Teacher Created Materials
5301 Oceanus Drive
Huntington Beach, CA 92649-1030
http://www.tcmpub.com
ISBN 978-1-4333-4906-5
© 2013 Teacher Created Materials, Inc.

TABLE OF CONTENTS

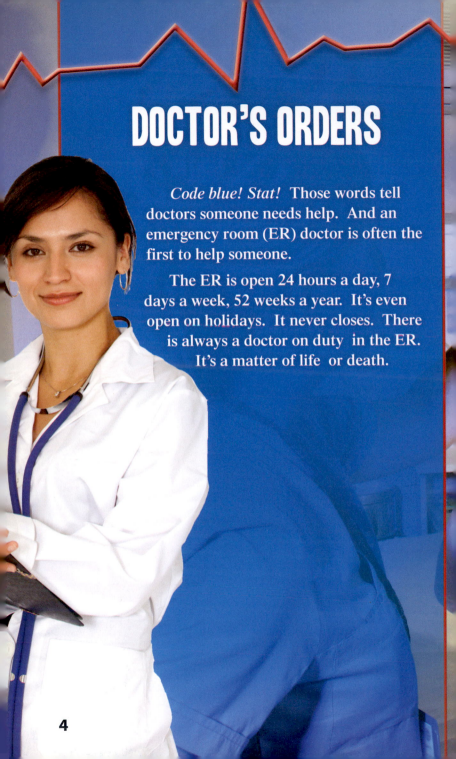

DOCTOR'S ORDERS

Code blue! Stat! Those words tell doctors someone needs help. And an emergency room (ER) doctor is often the first to help someone.

The ER is open 24 hours a day, 7 days a week, 52 weeks a year. It's even open on holidays. It never closes. There is always a doctor on duty in the ER. It's a matter of life or death.

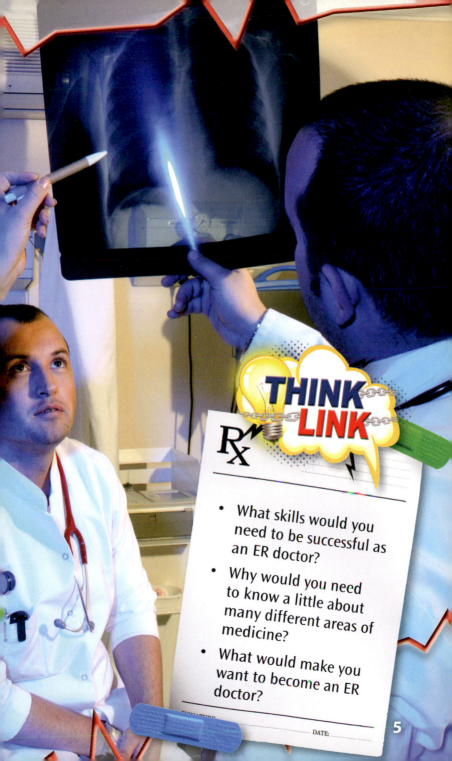

THINK LINK

R⃥x

- What skills would you need to be successful as an ER doctor?

- Why would you need to know a little about many different areas of medicine?

- What would make you want to become an ER doctor?

DATE:

FIRST THINGS FIRST

Arriving at the ER can be hectic. If a patient is ill, the last thing he or she wants to do is wait for **treatment**. But the ER is often filled with patients. Some of them may have woken up with a bad cold in the middle of the night. Others may have been in a car accident, suffered a heart attack, or taken a turn for the worse. In a regular doctor's office, people make an appointment to see the doctor. But in the ER, the doctor must treat the patients with the most serious **symptoms**—whenever they show up.

Triage nurses talk with each patient. They determine what kind of care each patient needs. They decide who needs help the most. If there are 10 patients and only one doctor, this process helps the doctor know who to treat first.

Patient Profiles

ER doctors work with everyone from young babies to seniors. They work with people who have the sniffles and people who are dying. ER doctors treat people who have been in car wrecks and people who have broken bones from falls or fights. They even deliver babies.

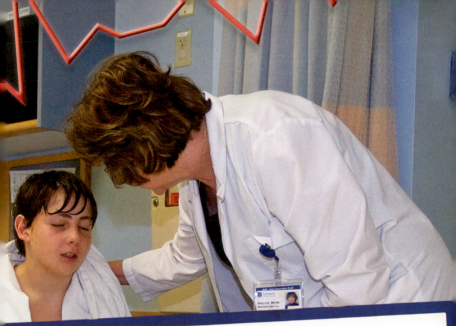

Trauma Centers

Some hospitals have **trauma** centers built to handle the worst injuries. Some trauma centers are equipped to handle serious surgeries, and some are not.

Level I	**Specialists** are available 24 hours a day. The hospital also offers in-house surgery, **anesthesia** (an-uhs-THEE-zhuh), and a research program. Being treated at a Level I center increases survival rates up to 25 percent.
Level II	These hospitals offer in-house anesthesia, specialists, and surgery, but no research programs.
Level III	This type of trauma center only offers surgery and anesthesia during certain hours. Only a few select specialists are available.
Level IV	These centers are located in rural areas. They are usually places where patients stop before moving on to more advanced trauma centers.

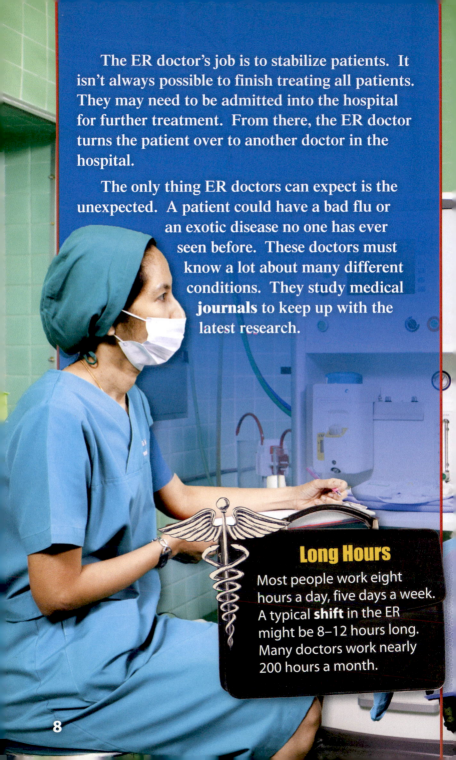

The ER doctor's job is to stabilize patients. It isn't always possible to finish treating all patients. They may need to be admitted into the hospital for further treatment. From there, the ER doctor turns the patient over to another doctor in the hospital.

The only thing ER doctors can expect is the unexpected. A patient could have a bad flu or an exotic disease no one has ever seen before. These doctors must know a lot about many different conditions. They study medical **journals** to keep up with the latest research.

Long Hours

Most people work eight hours a day, five days a week. A typical **shift** in the ER might be 8–12 hours long. Many doctors work nearly 200 hours a month.

Around the Clock Care

Doctors rarely know what to expect each day, so they plan for the unexpected. They start by going to the bathroom and eating right before they start working. They might not get another chance for the next 12 hours! A day in the ER may look something like this.

6:00 A.M.   Scope out the waiting room. The night doctor transfers patients to the next doctor on duty.

8:00 A.M.   **Rounds** begin. ER doctors must visit the sickest patients first.

9:00 A.M.   A Level 1 trauma patient is admitted. This patient is treated first because of the severity of the injury.

10:00 A.M.   Return to rounds. Check each patient's symptoms.

11:00 A.M.   Record notes for later use.

12:00 P.M.   Eat a few bites.

1:00 P.M.   Manage patients' needs as they get better or worse. Get lab results, discharge patients, and take medical histories.

5:00 P.M.   Give important information to the ER doctor starting the night shift.

6:00 P.M.   Go home, relax, spend time with friends and family.

DIG DEEPER!

Inside an Ambulance

When a person is too sick or injured to drive, an ambulance takes the patient to the ER. Ambulances can drive quickly and go through red lights. And if a patient needs surgery, the crew on board will call ahead to warn the ER. The doctors wait outside for the ambulance. In a trauma, every second counts.

Patients lie on a gurney during transport.

Air conditioning regulates the temperature and keeps the air clean.

A ramp lets drivers load patients and equipment without heavy lifting.

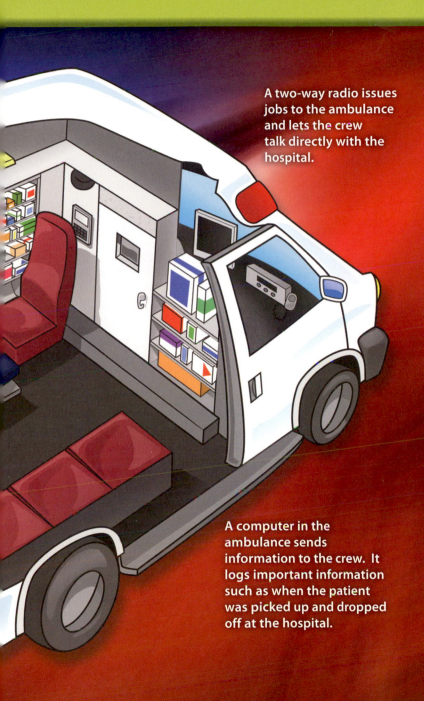

A two-way radio issues jobs to the ambulance and lets the crew talk directly with the hospital.

A computer in the ambulance sends information to the crew. It logs important information such as when the patient was picked up and dropped off at the hospital.

THINK FAST!

Across the country, ER doctors treat more than 100 million patients every year. Many of them come in for simple aches and pains. Some are serious cases, and others are not. But no matter what the symptoms are, doctors advise people to come in rather than to wait. It can be hard to know whether they are serious or not.

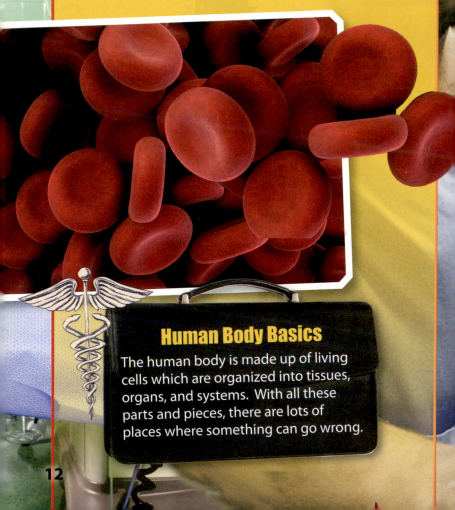

Human Body Basics

The human body is made up of living cells which are organized into tissues, organs, and systems. With all these parts and pieces, there are lots of places where something can go wrong.

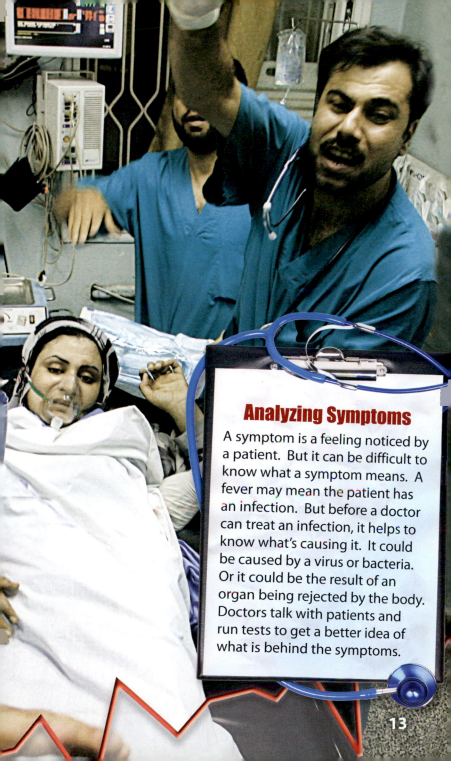

Analyzing Symptoms

A symptom is a feeling noticed by a patient. But it can be difficult to know what a symptom means. A fever may mean the patient has an infection. But before a doctor can treat an infection, it helps to know what's causing it. It could be caused by a virus or bacteria. Or it could be the result of an organ being rejected by the body. Doctors talk with patients and run tests to get a better idea of what is behind the symptoms.

RUNNING TESTS

Each symptom is a piece of the puzzle. But symptoms alone aren't enough to know why a patient is ill. Symptoms help doctors treat patients. But without more information, the symptoms can also mislead doctors. That's why it's important to run tests.

Radiology tests use images to look for problems in the body. X-rays, MRIs, and CAT scans are all examples of radiology tests.

A urinalysis uses a patient's urine. Doctors look to see if there is blood, bacteria, or protein in the urine. They look for metals and other molecules.

Blood tests require samples taken from a patient's vein using a needle. Doctors know what healthy blood readings look like. If there is a problem, the blood sample will reveal it.

What's Next?

When the results are in, the doctor decides how to proceed. If the results are good, the patient may not need further treatment. Or the patient may need to see a specialist. Other times, test results will show a patient needs surgery immediately.

A SERIOUS ILLNESS

It's 2 A.M. and a three-month-old baby arrives in the ER with a fever of 101°F. The baby isn't sleeping or eating. Fevers can be very dangerous in young children. A high fever can even cause a **seizure** and other health complications. ER doctors treat babies with high fevers right away. They also treat the other cold-like symptoms that may accompany a high fever.

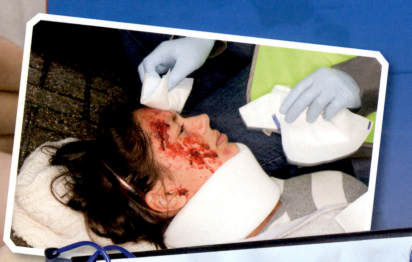

Common Complaints

Below are the leading reasons children and adults visit the ER. When in doubt, doctors agree it is best to get an expert opinion, even in the middle of the night.

Children
- high fevers
- earaches
- broken bones

Adults
- heart attacks
- stomach pain
- back pain
- injuries from a fall

Fever is one way the human body fights infection. A fever activates the immune system.

WICKED WOUNDS

Next up may be a boy who was injured riding his bike. Perhaps a car slammed into him. Thrown from his bike, the boy may have hit a nearby tree. He could even have fallen **unconscious**, with a thick tree branch wedged into his stomach. In the ER, the nurses try to control the bleeding. They assess the wound and call the doctors in. Best-case **scenario**: he needs stitches. Worst-case scenario: the branch hit an organ. In that case, the doctor may need to perform surgery. And the boy's family will be hoping the injuries won't be **fatal**.

Simple Stitches

ER doctors sew up cuts when someone has been hurt. The thread they use for sewing is different than the kind you might use at home when sewing a button on your clothes. They use thread that looks like fishing line. These **sutures**, or stitches, help the body heal.

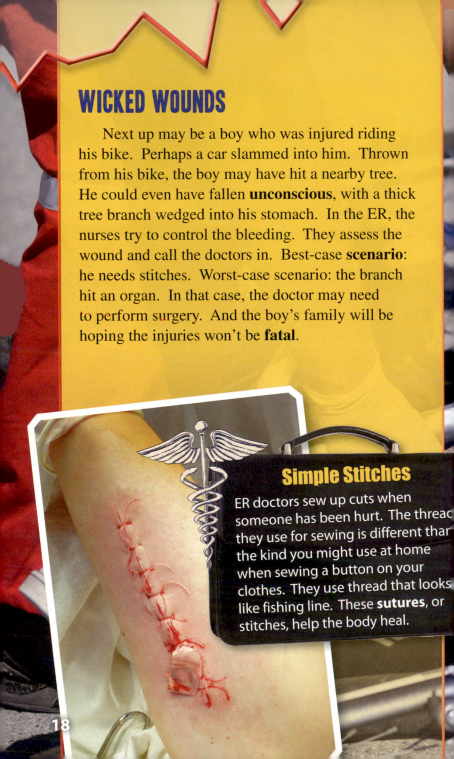

Shocking

A wound can be fatal if the victim goes into **shock**. It can happen when someone loses a lot of blood, an infection develops, or organs, such as the heart or lungs, fail.

PAINFUL PROBLEMS

Doctors in the ER often care for people who are in pain. Sometimes, it's obvious what's causing the pain. It's hard to miss a knife sticking out of someone's hand! But other times, even the patient may not know where the pain is coming from.

Doctors treat these patients with pain medicine. But the cause of the problem may still be unclear. The ER doctor's main job is to make sure the patient lives. Once the patient is stable, it's time to send the patient home or on to the next doctor. It's common for ER doctors to refer most of their patients to specialists.

Finding a Bed

If it's not a matter of life or death, patients may wait for hours to be seen. Nurses try to find safe, comfortable places for patients to wait. When hospitals are crowded, it can be difficult to find a bed for a patient. And if a bed is found, it might be even harder to find where to put it. If hospital rooms are filled, beds may be placed in hallways.

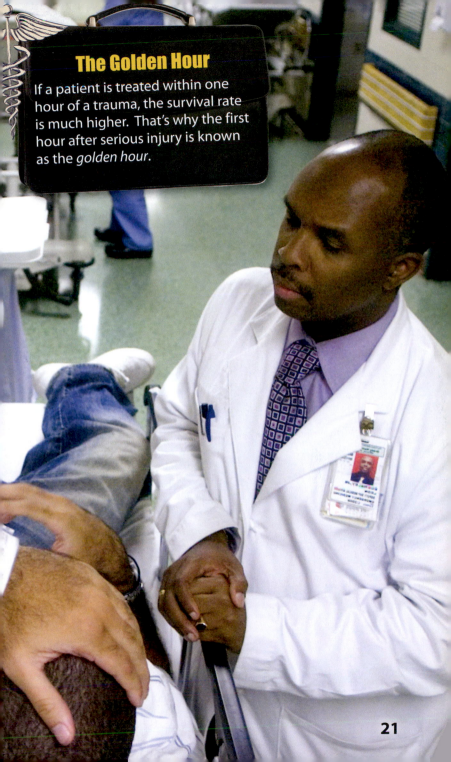

The Golden Hour

If a patient is treated within one hour of a trauma, the survival rate is much higher. That's why the first hour after serious injury is known as the *golden hour*.

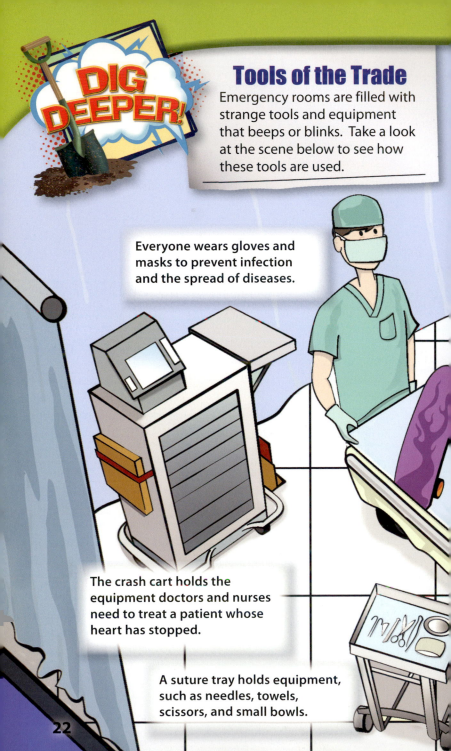

DIG DEEPER!

Tools of the Trade

Emergency rooms are filled with strange tools and equipment that beeps or blinks. Take a look at the scene below to see how these tools are used.

Everyone wears gloves and masks to prevent infection and the spread of diseases.

The crash cart holds the equipment doctors and nurses need to treat a patient whose heart has stopped.

A suture tray holds equipment, such as needles, towels, scissors, and small bowls.

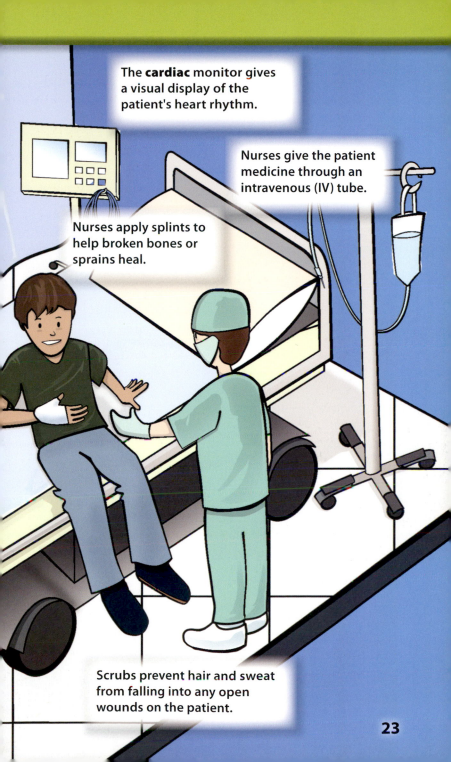

The **cardiac** monitor gives a visual display of the patient's heart rhythm.

Nurses give the patient medicine through an intravenous (IV) tube.

Nurses apply splints to help broken bones or sprains heal.

Scrubs prevent hair and sweat from falling into any open wounds on the patient.

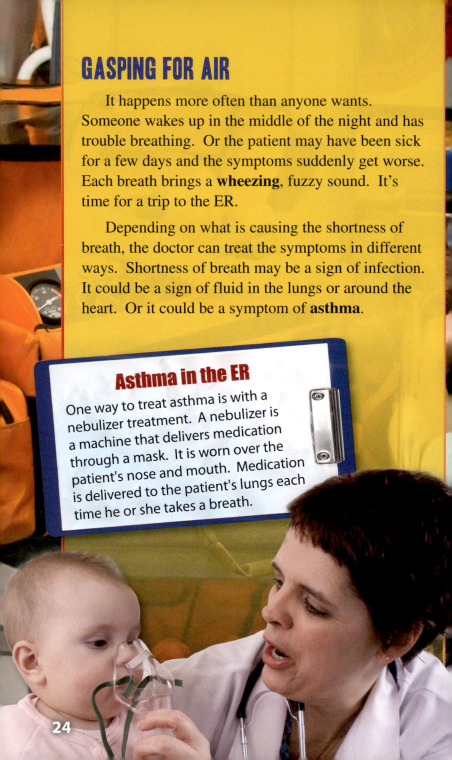

GASPING FOR AIR

It happens more often than anyone wants. Someone wakes up in the middle of the night and has trouble breathing. Or the patient may have been sick for a few days and the symptoms suddenly get worse. Each breath brings a **wheezing**, fuzzy sound. It's time for a trip to the ER.

Depending on what is causing the shortness of breath, the doctor can treat the symptoms in different ways. Shortness of breath may be a sign of infection. It could be a sign of fluid in the lungs or around the heart. Or it could be a symptom of **asthma**.

Asthma in the ER

One way to treat asthma is with a nebulizer treatment. A nebulizer is a machine that delivers medication through a mask. It is worn over the patient's nose and mouth. Medication is delivered to the patient's lungs each time he or she takes a breath.

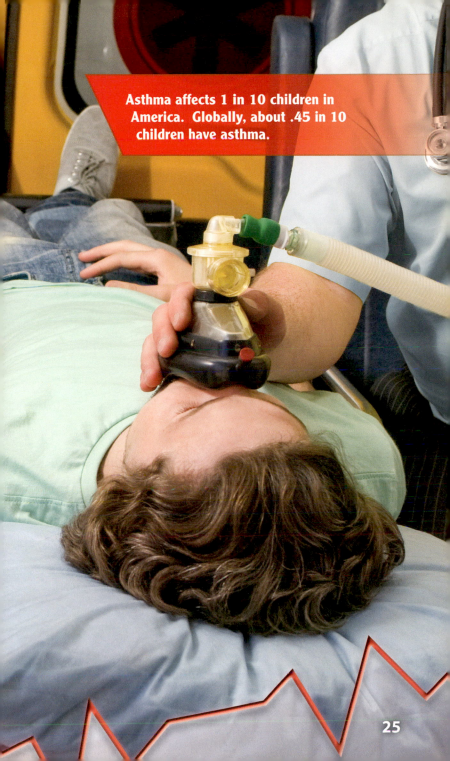

Asthma affects 1 in 10 children in America. Globally, about .45 in 10 children have asthma.

THE INVISIBLE INJURY

A woman may arrive after **fainting** and hitting her head. She may feel weak and confused. The triage nurse will move her to the front of the line.

Head injuries are known as *invisible injuries.* They are hard to diagnose and treat. They may cause cracks in the skull, bruises in the brain, and **concussions**. These invisible injuries can even lead to death. ER doctors test patients' speech, memory, movement, and reasoning. Minor head injuries may simply require rest. Major injuries, which could involve brain damage, may take months or years to recover from.

In the areas of the world with very good medical care, 25 in 100,000 head injuries end in death.

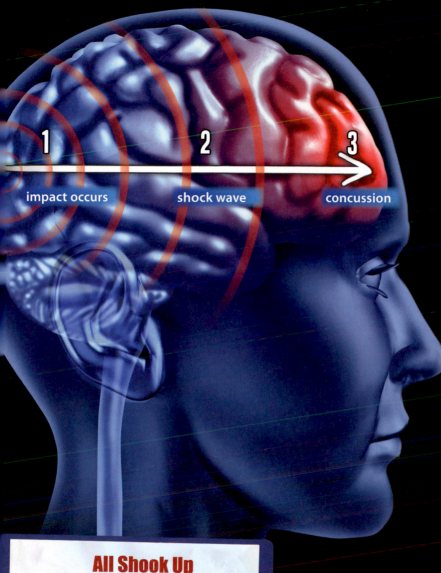

1 impact occurs **2** shock wave **3** concussion

All Shook Up

A concussion can occur when the brain is shaken. It's a common football injury. Sometimes, it occurs during a car accident. Nerves and blood vessels in the brain can tear during trauma.

Look Inside

Doctors use a variety of machines to "see" inside the human body. They choose what tests to run based on the patient's symptoms. X-rays are commonly used to see if a bone is broken. Scans are used when head injuries are suspected.

Test	Result	Purpose
X-Ray	a single picture	show bones
Computed Tomography (CT-Scan or CAT-Scan)	multiple pictures of many layers	show bones and can detect **cancer**
Magnetic Resonance Imaging (MRI)	multiple pictures of many layers from different angles	show soft tissues such as eyes, look for **tumors** or signs of a **stroke**

Method	Time	Cost	Pros	Cons
patient is carefully positioned so only the body part in question is tested	seconds	least expensive	very quick	exposes the patient to **radiation**; image is only from one perspective
patient lies very still on a table that slides into a machine	five minutes	moderately expensive	quicker and less expensive than an MRI	exposes the patient to radiation; more expensive than an X-ray; images are only from one direction
patient lies on a table that slides into a machine	over half an hour	very expensive	most accurate and shows the most useful information	takes a long time, requiring the patient to be still in a confined place; being in the machine can be noisy and scary for the patient

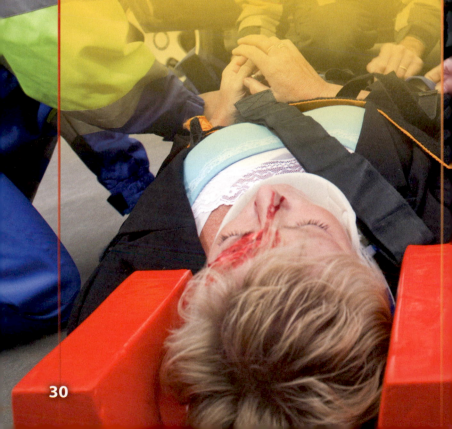

ACCIDENTS

Later in the shift, an ambulance may arrive with sirens screeching. Maybe there's been a car accident. The victim could be bleeding and having trouble breathing. The other driver could be coming in the next ambulance.

ER doctors see many people who have been in car wrecks. Most people who are hurt badly were not wearing their seat belts. Injuries can happen even if a seat belt is worn, but they can be much worse without one. Simple decisions can save someone's life.

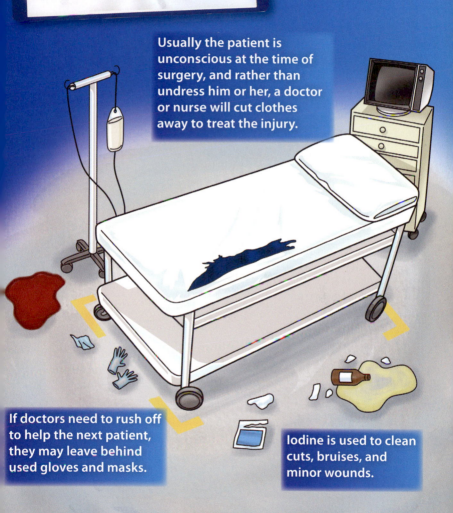

Traumatic Debris

If there is a lot of blood, the ER team will do its best to contain it. But everyone's primary concern is treating the patient, not the mess at their feet.

Usually the patient is unconscious at the time of surgery, and rather than undress him or her, a doctor or nurse will cut clothes away to treat the injury.

If doctors need to rush off to help the next patient, they may leave behind used gloves and masks.

Iodine is used to clean cuts, bruises, and minor wounds.

31

Checking the Chart

The chart includes all the patient's most important health information. It notes past illnesses and injuries, test results, and the doctor's **diagnosis**. Any member of the ER team can look at the chart to check on the patient's condition. Look below to see a sample medical chart.

Jane Doe

Date: 04/19/2012   **Doctor:** Dr. Torrey N. Smith

Patient Name: Jane Doe

ADMITTED

○ Male   ● Female

DOB: 05/11/1999

Allergies: none

Routine Medications: daily use of an inhaler

Reason for Visit: Jane arrived with shortness of breath and wheezing. Went to sleep without symptoms and woke up unable to breathe with an intense wheeze. Repeated history of asthma. Last treated ~~asthma~~ by our medical facilities in 2011.

℞

PATIENT NAME Jane Doe
ADDRESS:
1234 Sick St.
Townsville, CA 98765

Use inhaler daily.

Dr. Smith

STOP! THINK...

- What are the patient's symptoms?

- Has the doctor designed a treatment plan?

- Do you think the patient will go home soon?

Height: *58"*

Weight: *90 pounds*

Pulse: *60*

Blood Pressure: *110/75*

Labs: *Tests are pending.*

Assessment: *minor asthma attack*

PENDING

Plan: *treated with nebulizer, will recheck patient, call if symptoms worsen.*

Pending Labs: *hemogram, urinalysis, basic, lipids, SGOT, CPK, stool for hemoccult*

Next Appointment: *follow up in six months*

RUNNING A CODE

A patient may seem to be improving and then take a turn for the worse. Suddenly, she may not be able to speak. She may have trouble breathing.

When a patient's heart stops, every second counts. A code blue is announced. The team works together to perform **cardiopulmonary resuscitation (CPR)** (ri-SUHS-i-TEY-shun). One doctor runs the code by telling everyone else what to do. Another doctor works on the patient. One nurse records what's happening. Another nurse prepares medicines. Someone pumps air into the patient's mouth and nose. A nurse presses on the patient's chest to try to get the heart pumping again. A **defibrillator** is used to shock the heart with electricity.

Speaking in Code

Codes can vary from hospital to hospital but here are some ways that conditions are reported.

code blue—a patient's heart has stopped and needs CPR

code pink—a baby or patient is missing

code red—fire

code brown—a patient soiled the bed

code green—violent patient; send security

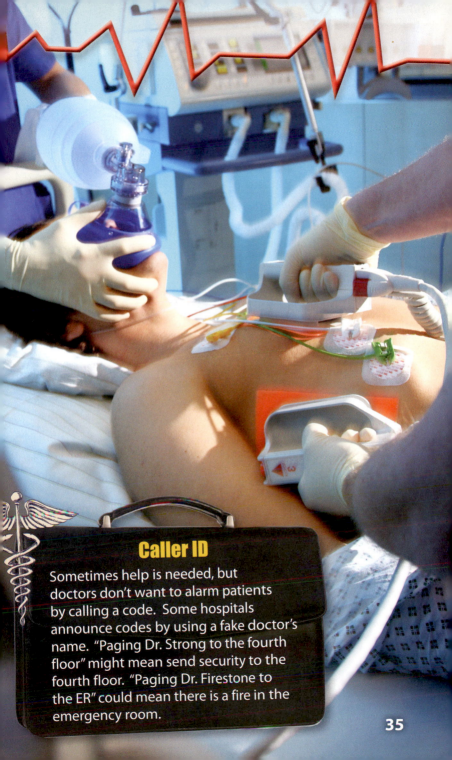

Caller ID

Sometimes help is needed, but doctors don't want to alarm patients by calling a code. Some hospitals announce codes by using a fake doctor's name. "Paging Dr. Strong to the fourth floor" might mean send security to the fourth floor. "Paging Dr. Firestone to the ER" could mean there is a fire in the emergency room.

SLAMMED

Just when the ER is starting to clear out, a disaster may strike. Maybe a large earthquake hits. The hospital is still standing, but buildings may fall and fires may break out. Patients will stream in at a steady rate. Some will have minor cuts. Others could have major burns. The halls could be overflowing.

During a natural disaster, hospitals may need to admit large numbers of patients. Many schools have fire drills so they know what to do during a fire. Hospitals have drills as well. They train so everyone knows what to do during a disaster.

A Chinese hospital grows crowded during a disaster.

Get in Gear

Even in the chaos of an ER, it's easy to recognize a doctor. Each piece of clothing and every tool is used to treat patients and make doctors as efficient as possible.

Doctors wear white coats over scrubs. Scrubs can be changed easily if blood gets on them. Coats are washed after each shift.

A stethoscope allows doctors to listen to the heart and lungs.

A watch with a second hand measures patients' heart rates.

The length of the coat may signal whether the doctor is still a student or more experienced.

Each doctor has his or her own pad to order **prescriptions**. A pharmacy won't fill a prescription unless it's written on an official piece of paper and signed by a doctor.

Doctors always carry pens to write down observations and instructions for the nurses.

DIG DEEPER!

By the Numbers

A typical week in a hospital might include the following patients. Of course, no week is really typical.

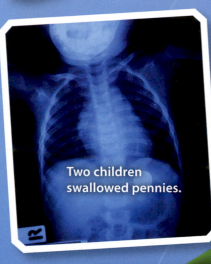

Two children swallowed pennies.

Four children come in with broken bones.

Eight people complain of bad digestion.

One man broke off
a pencil in his ear.

Ten people are
treated for strokes.

Seven patients have
trouble breathing.

Nine patients suffer
heart attacks.

**Average cost
of an ER visit:**

$707

**Average time spent
in the ER:**

4 hours,
5 minutes

**Number of
ambulances per year
sent to a different
hospital due to lack of
staff and space:**

500,000

STRANGE MEDICINE

Sometimes, the ER may grow quiet. Some days are dramatic. But other days can only be described as strange. What else would you call it when a woman complains of severe stomach pains and an X-ray shows she has swallowed over 50 pieces of silverware? What about a man who falls off a ladder only to have a long hook pierce his eyeball? Or a woman may rush to the ER with extreme abdominal pain. Without knowing it, she's nearly nine months pregnant. Soon, she will deliver a baby girl or boy. Patients arrive at the ER with all kinds of strange stories. Unfortunately, that doesn't make their injuries any less painful! But it might be something they can laugh about later.

Nearly 2,500 people take a trip to the ER every year because of injuries caused by toothbrushes! Most of the injuries occur because someone falls while brushing.

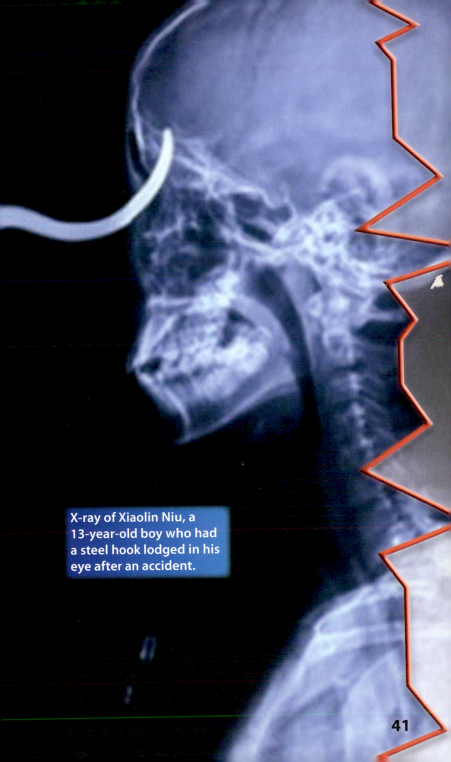

X-ray of Xiaolin Niu, a 13-year-old boy who had a steel hook lodged in his eye after an accident.

DIG DEEPER!

Where To?

After a patient is treated by an ER doctor, he or she may be sent to a different department within the hospital. Age, illnesses, and injuries play a large role in determining which ward the patient should be transferred to.

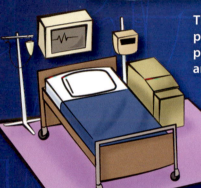

The intensive care unit provides constant care to patients whose conditions are life threatening.

The coronary care unit treats patients who have had heart attacks and other heart trouble.

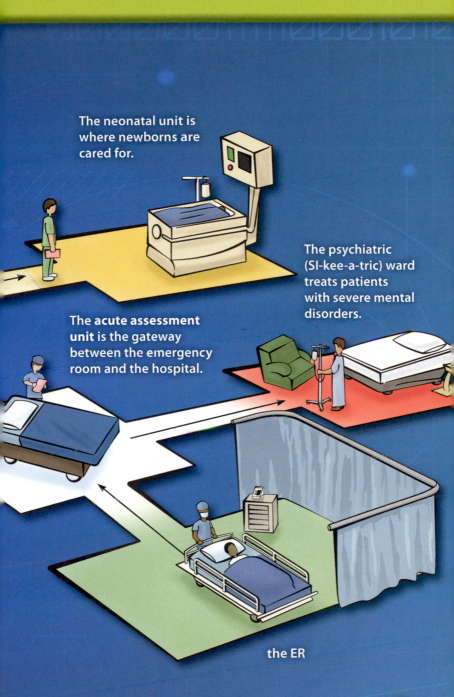

The neonatal unit is where newborns are cared for.

The psychiatric (SI-kee-a-tric) ward treats patients with severe mental disorders.

The **acute assessment unit** is the gateway between the emergency room and the hospital.

the ER

OVER AND OUT

When the shift is over, it's time to relax. Working 12 hours is tough, but ER doctors are used to it. And when the days are busy, they may not even notice the hours ticking by.

At the end of the shift, the doctor on duty lets the next doctor know which patients need help first. The patient charts must be updated. The notes need to be detailed to include everything that happened. Leaving out the smallest detail could affect the way the next doctor treats a patient's illness. The next doctor must be able to take over and finish any case that was started earlier.

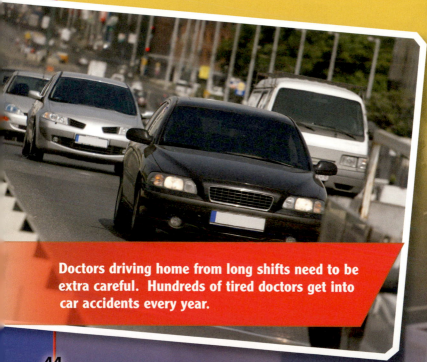

Doctors driving home from long shifts need to be extra careful. Hundreds of tired doctors get into car accidents every year.

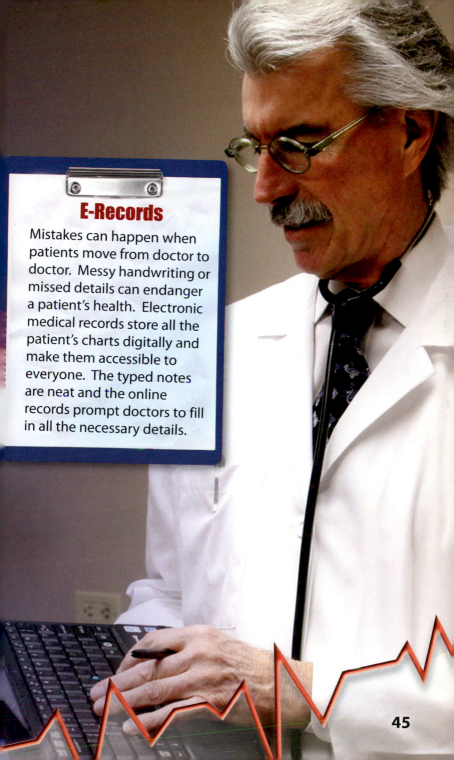

E-Records

Mistakes can happen when patients move from doctor to doctor. Messy handwriting or missed details can endanger a patient's health. Electronic medical records store all the patient's charts digitally and make them accessible to everyone. The typed notes are neat and the online records prompt doctors to fill in all the necessary details.

LEARNING TO HEAL

Like all doctors, ER doctors aren't afraid of blood, and they like helping people. They think like scientists. And they know how to communicate with patients. ER doctors must also be able to think quickly. Working on their feet for long hours comes with the territory. They must know what questions to ask and pay close attention to patients' responses. It's essential that they stay calm. They must be willing to take control in stressful situations. Lives depend on them.

Try It

In high school, students can volunteer to help people in the lab, the ER, or in the waiting rooms. This is a good way to see how the hospital works. Older students can work as orderlies or nursing assistants. These people help feed, bathe, and clothe patients. They also transport patients to their tests and help them walk in the halls.

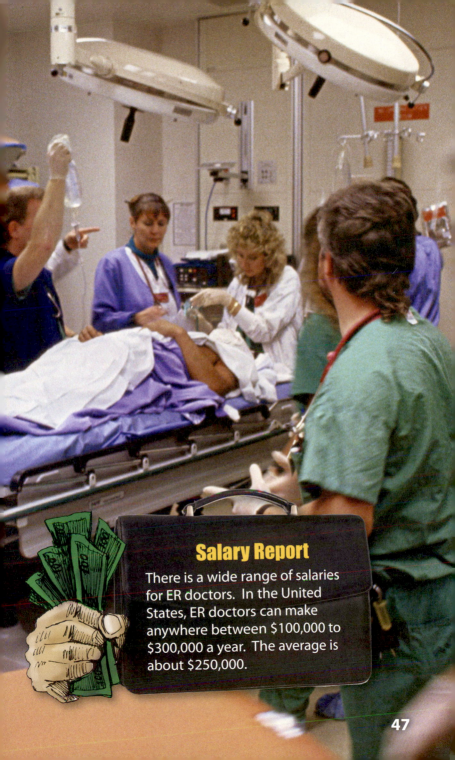

Salary Report

There is a wide range of salaries for ER doctors. In the United States, ER doctors can make anywhere between $100,000 to $300,000 a year. The average is about $250,000.

HITTING THE BOOKS

It takes a lot of hard work to become a doctor. Students interested in this career must do well in high school and college. Those who are thinking about becoming doctors should study biology, chemistry, and physics. Some students become pre-med majors in college. This means they intend to go to medical school and will focus on science and math in college. Other students explore other passions and majors before medical school.

After college, they must attend several more years of medical school. The competition is tough. Medical school provides each student with a strong understanding of biology, medicine, diseases, parts of the body, and how to talk with patients. The first two years of medical school are spent learning about science. Students study a **cadaver** (kuh-DAV-er) to learn about the different parts of the body. Textbooks teach them about diseases and injuries. The students must know what treatments will work for each condition. They may use computer programs and models to practice their skills.

Students first practice listening for patients' heartbeats by using a doll.

Medical school is tough but more than 96 percent of medical students go on to receive their degrees.

The next two years are spent studying in hospitals and clinics. Students learn about all the different areas of medicine. As they begin to treat patients, they learn more every day.

When students complete medical school, they are officially doctors. But these new doctors still need to choose a specialty. During **residency**, doctors learn more about an area of medicine. An ER doctor focuses on emergency medicine during residency.

After completing residency, doctors need a special license to practice medicine. They get the license from the state they plan to practice in. They must also pass a licensing exam. Even though they have their licenses, doctors continue learning throughout their lives. They attend conferences and workshops to learn how other doctors are treating patients. They want to learn about the latest advances in the field.

A Fast Learner

Medical students are expected to learn new skills quickly. "See one, do one, teach one" is a saying in medicine. It's a quick way to describe how students learn medical procedures.

First, students watch more experienced doctors perform the procedure.

Do

Then, they try doing it as a senior doctor watches nearby.

Teach

Eventually, they will teach new students the same skills.

51

SAVING LIVES

Doctors in the ER can hold a human heart in their hands, deliver a baby, and bind broken bones. They often see patients at their weakest moments. But when it's a matter of life or death, patients are grateful these doctors are there to make decisions. Doctors can't heal every patient, but they know it's an honor to try.

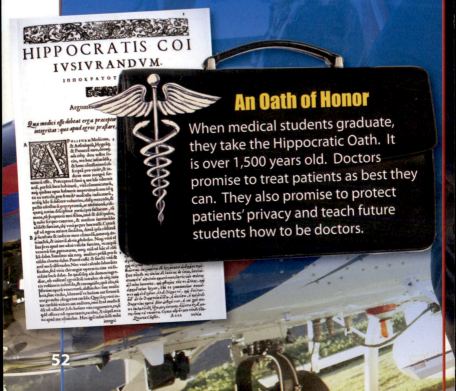

An Oath of Honor

When medical students graduate, they take the Hippocratic Oath. It is over 1,500 years old. Doctors promise to treat patients as best they can. They also promise to protect patients' privacy and teach future students how to be doctors.

Good Intentions

Many doctors hold themselves to another more casual oath. They promise they will try to "do no harm." Holding themselves to this standard can help them make decisions about what kinds of risks to take when treating a patient.

After a lifetime of study, events in the ER can happen in a flash. If things go badly, an ER doctor's face may be the last face a patient sees. But these doctors fight every day to make sure that doesn't happen. They dedicate themselves to keeping their patients alive. They take it hard when someone doesn't survive. But soon it will be time to treat a new patient. In the ER, there is always another life to save.

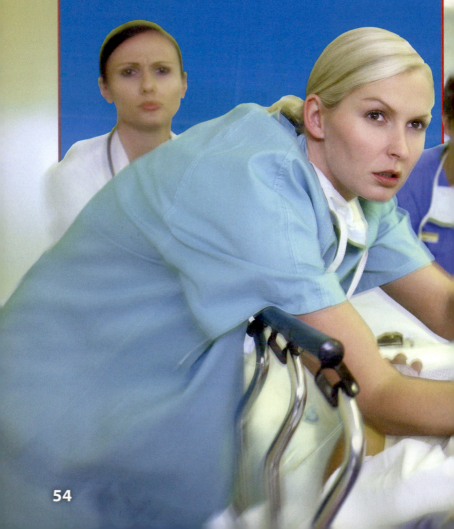

Meet an ER Doctor

Meet Dr. Byron Garibaldi. He is an ER doctor at Northwest Medical Center in Springdale, Arkansas. His official title is staff ER doctor. He has been a doctor for more than 15 years. Like any ER doctor, he had some amazing stories to tell writer Diana Herweck.

Diana: Why did you want to become a doctor?

Dr. Garibaldi: Initially, I really wanted to be a pilot like my father, who was a pilot for almost 30 years. But, my eyesight grew worse. A military flying career was fading fast. In my junior year of high school, I decided I wanted to be a doctor, since it was a noble profession that many people respected, and took hard work to achieve. I was hoping it paid well and I could support a family well on my income.

Diana: Did your training prepare you for the job?

Dr. Garibaldi: Yes! As residents, we helped with most surgeries, delivering babies, working the hospital medical floor, intensive care work, working in the ER, and taking care of clinic patients. If there was a medical problem to take care of, we were there. It was a great residency, because the private practice doctors took a ton of time to teach us all they could.

Diana: What would you tell someone who is interested in becoming an ER doctor?

Dr. Garibaldi: Try volunteering to do odd jobs in the ER and see if it is the right place for you or not. The ER is completely different than any place in the hospital. You are dealing with sick and unusual people all the time. If you need structure, the ER is not the place for you. You need to adapt quickly in the ER.

Diana: What's your favorite part of working in the ER?

Dr. Garibaldi: My absolute favorite part of the ER is the **camaraderie** between the doctors, nurses, and techs that I work with. We are usually laughing and playing practical jokes on one another in between patients. It certainly breaks up the stress of the job. I also like that you never know what will come through the door. It may be the sickest patient you have ever seen or the most unusual sickness or problem you have ever taken care of. Those are the patients that stick with you for a lifetime.

GLOSSARY

acute assessment unit—a department in some hospitals that acts as a gateway between a patient's doctor, the emergency department, and the wards of the hospital

anesthesia—medicine that causes a loss of sensation in the body and possibly a loss of consciousness

asthma—a condition that is marked by difficulty breathing, coughing, and tightness in the chest

cadaver—the dead body of a person

camaraderie—good feelings between people in a group

cancer—a disease that can cause tissue to grow abnormally and often causes death if not treated

cardiac—relating to the heart

cardiopulmonary resuscitation (CPR)—a series of steps used to restore normal breathing and heart rhythm when the heart stops

concussions—injuries in the brain resulting from a sudden impact to the body

defibrillator—a machine that delivers an electric shock to restore the heart's normal rhythm

diagnosis—the identification of a disease based on a patient's symptoms and test results

fainting—losing consciousness

fatal—causing death

journals—magazines that report new research to a specific group of people such as doctors

prescriptions—written instructions from a doctor for a patient's medicine or other treatment

radiation—powerful waves or particles of energy; used to capture images of bones and internal organs

residency—a period of advanced training that typically follows graduation from medical school

rounds—a series of visits to hospital patients made by doctors each day

scenario—a description of what could possibly happen

seizure—an episode of abnormal brain activity that can produce uncontrollable shaking in the body

shift—the period of time during which workers are scheduled to work

shock—a dangerous condition caused by severe injuries in which the body fails to pump blood to all the necessary areas and becomes weakened

specialists—people who are experts on a specific area of medicine

stroke—the death of brain cells resulting from poor blood flow

sutures—strands or fibers used to sew together parts of the body

symptoms—a change that indicates the presence of a disease or other physical disorder, especially one that can be felt or sensed by a patient

trauma—a serious injury to a person's body

treatment—the use of medicines, surgery, or other methods to address a medical condition

triage—to sort patients into categories depending on who is likely to survive, those who can wait for treatment, and those who need treatment immediately

tumors—a mass of tissue found in or on the body that is made up of abnormal cells

unconscious—having lost awareness and the ability to think

wheezing—breathing with difficulty especially with a whistling sound

INDEX

BIBLIOGRAPHY

Buhler Gale, Karen. *The Kids' Guide to First Aid.* **Williamson Publishing Company, 2001.**

Test your medical skills in safe and easy ways with this book. Learn how to treat basic bruises, burns, stings, sprains, and splinters. But always visit an ER if you run into serious trouble.

Lang, Rocky and Erick Montero. *Confessions of Emergency Room Doctors.* **Andrews McMeel Publishing, 2007.**

Find out the weird, wild, and wonderful things that happen in ERs straight from the doctors who work there. This book contains strange, funny, and totally true stories about life in the ER.

Lewis, Barbara A. *The Kid's Guide to Service Projects: Over 500 Service Ideas for Young People Who Want to Make a Difference, 2nd edition.* **Free Spirit Publishing, 2009.**

You're not an ER doctor, nurse, or paramedic yet, but it's never too soon to help out. Try one of the service project ideas in this book to promote healthy habits, prevent diseases, or make a difference in your neighborhood in some other way.

Reeves, Diane L. *Career Ideas for Kids Who Like Science.* **Checkmark Books, 2007.**

Find the right career by answering questions that help you find what you like to do and what you do best. You can link your hobbies and skills to real careers. Interviews with professionals, ranging from a medical technologist and a food scientist to a robotics consultant and a veterinarian, help you discover what careers in science are really like.

MORE TO EXPLORE

Emergency Room Nurse
http://www.knowitall.scetv.org/careeraisle/clusters/index.cfm

Click the *Health Science* link. Then, click the *Emergency Room Nurse* link. Take a tour through the emergency room with an ER nurse. She'll show you how to get admitted, what happens in the triage room and trauma bay, and how different ER equipment works. She also describes the various hospital workers in the ER, including trauma doctors, nurses, and X-ray technicians.

Kids Work! Hospital
http://www.knowitall.org/kidswork/hospital/index.html

Learn about the history of hospitals, play activities that show how schoolwork relates to hospital work, and explore workplaces in a hospital. You'll also meet real-life hospital professionals, including a trauma surgeon, medical lab technician, and neonatal nurse.

What Happens in the Emergency Room?
http://www.kidshealth.org/kid/feel_better/places/er.html

Read this KidsHealth article to find out what happens step by step when kids go to the emergency room. You'll also learn some useful "ER Talk" terms that ER doctors and nurses use.

Doctor
http://www.bls.gov/k12/help06.htm

This website helps you explore career information from the Bureau of Labor Statistics. Get the latest numbers on how much doctors are paid, how many jobs are out there, and the future of employment for doctors, physicians, and surgeons.

ABOUT THE AUTHOR

Diana Herweck has always been interested in the things people do, including their jobs. She works as a teacher and a counselor, helping people of all ages decide what they want to do when they grow up. Just like doctors, she enjoys helping people. She also loves working with children and spending time with her family. She enjoys playing with her kids, reading, music, movies, and crafts of all sorts, especially scrapbooking. Diana lives in Southern California with her husband, two wonderful children, and three dogs.